BUSINESS BUDGET PLANNER FOR SMALL SERVICE BASED BUSINESSES

COMPANY NAME _____

TELEPHONE _____

E-MAIL _____

JANUARY BUDGET

YEAR:

SOURCES OF INCOME SUMMARY	PROJECTED	ACTUAL	DIFFERENCE (+/-)
EXPENSES			
SAVINGS			
OTHER			

MONTHLY EXPENSE SUMMARY	PROJECTED	ACTUAL	DIFFERENCE (+/-)

JANUARY INCOME

DATE	SALES SOURCE	$ INCOME

JANUARY INCOME

DATE	SALES SOURCE	$ INCOME

JANUARY INCOME

DATE	SALES SOURCE	$ INCOME

JANUARY EXPENSES

DATE	DESCRIPTION	$ AMOUNT

JANUARY EXPENSES

DATE	DESCRIPTION	$ AMOUNT

JANUARY BUSINESS GOALS

_____

_____

_____

_____

_____

_____

_____

JANUARY MARKETING PLAN

CAMPAIGN/AUDIENCE	COST	NOTES

JANUARY SUPPLY INVENTORY

QTY	ITEM	$ VALUE	REORDER DATE	REORDER QTY	NOTES

FEBRUARY BUDGET

YEAR:

SOURCES OF INCOME SUMMARY	PROJECTED	ACTUAL	DIFFERENCE (+/-)
EXPENSES			
SAVINGS			
OTHER			

MONTHLY EXPENSE SUMMARY	PROJECTED	ACTUAL	DIFFERENCE (+/-)

FEBRUARY INCOME

DATE	SALES SOURCE	$ INCOME

FEBRUARY INCOME

DATE	SALES SOURCE	$ INCOME

FEBRUARY INCOME

DATE	SALES SOURCE	$ INCOME

FEBRUARY EXPENSES

DATE	DESCRIPTION	$ AMOUNT

FEBRUARY EXPENSES

DATE	DESCRIPTION	$ AMOUNT

FEBRUARY BUSINESS GOALS

_____

_____

_____

_____

_____

_____

FEBRUARY MARKETING PLAN

CAMPAIGN/AUDIENCE	COST	NOTES

FEBRUARY SUPPLY INVENTORY

QTY	ITEM	$ VALUE	REORDER DATE	REORDER QTY	NOTES

MARCH BUDGET

YEAR:

SOURCES OF INCOME SUMMARY	PROJECTED	ACTUAL	DIFFERENCE (+/-)
EXPENSES			
SAVINGS			
OTHER			

MONTHLY EXPENSE SUMMARY	PROJECTED	ACTUAL	DIFFERENCE (+/-)

MARCH INCOME

DATE	SALES SOURCE	$ INCOME

MARCH INCOME

DATE	SALES SOURCE	$ INCOME

MARCH INCOME

DATE	SALES SOURCE	$ INCOME

MARCH EXPENSES

DATE	DESCRIPTION	$ AMOUNT

MARCH EXPENSES

DATE	DESCRIPTION	$ AMOUNT

MARCH BUSINESS GOALS

_____

_____

_____

_____

_____

_____

_____

MARCH MARKETING PLAN

CAMPAIGN/AUDIENCE	COST	NOTES

MARCH SUPPLY INVENTORY

QTY	ITEM	$ VALUE	REORDER DATE	REORDER QTY	NOTES

APRIL BUDGET

YEAR:

SOURCES OF INCOME SUMMARY	PROJECTED	ACTUAL	DIFFERENCE (+/-)
EXPENSES			
SAVINGS			
OTHER			

MONTHLY EXPENSE SUMMARY	PROJECTED	ACTUAL	DIFFERENCE (+/-)

APRIL INCOME

DATE	SALES SOURCE	$ INCOME

APRIL INCOME

DATE	SALES SOURCE	$ INCOME

APRIL INCOME

DATE	SALES SOURCE	$ INCOME

APRIL EXPENSES

DATE	DESCRIPTION	$ AMOUNT

APRIL EXPENSES

DATE	DESCRIPTION	$ AMOUNT

APRIL BUSINESS GOALS

_____

_____

_____

_____

_____

_____

_____

APRIL MARKETING PLAN

CAMPAIGN/AUDIENCE	COST	NOTES

APRIL SUPPLY INVENTORY

QTY	ITEM	$ VALUE	REORDER DATE	REORDER QTY	NOTES

MAY BUDGET

YEAR:

SOURCES OF INCOME SUMMARY	PROJECTED	ACTUAL	DIFFERENCE (+/-)
EXPENSES			
SAVINGS			
OTHER			

MONTHLY EXPENSE SUMMARY	PROJECTED	ACTUAL	DIFFERENCE (+/-)

MAY INCOME

DATE	SALES SOURCE	$ INCOME

MAY INCOME

DATE	SALES SOURCE	$ INCOME

MAY INCOME

DATE	SALES SOURCE	$ INCOME

MAY EXPENSES

DATE	DESCRIPTION	$ AMOUNT

MAY EXPENSES

DATE	DESCRIPTION	$ AMOUNT

MAY BUSINESS GOALS

_____

_____

_____

_____

_____

_____

MAY MARKETING PLAN

CAMPAIGN/AUDIENCE	COST	NOTES

MAY SUPPLY INVENTORY

QTY	ITEM	$ VALUE	REORDER DATE	REORDER QTY	NOTES

JUNE BUDGET

YEAR:

SOURCES OF INCOME SUMMARY	PROJECTED	ACTUAL	DIFFERENCE (+/-)
EXPENSES			
SAVINGS			
OTHER			

MONTHLY EXPENSE SUMMARY	PROJECTED	ACTUAL	DIFFERENCE (+/-)

JUNE INCOME

DATE	SALES SOURCE	$ INCOME

JUNE INCOME

DATE	SALES SOURCE	$ INCOME

JUNE INCOME

DATE	SALES SOURCE	$ INCOME

JUNE EXPENSES

DATE	DESCRIPTION	$ AMOUNT

JUNE EXPENSES

DATE	DESCRIPTION	$ AMOUNT

JUNE BUSINESS GOALS

_____

_____

_____

_____

_____

_____

_____

JUNE MARKETING PLAN

CAMPAIGN/AUDIENCE	COST	NOTES

JUNE SUPPLY INVENTORY

QTY	ITEM	$ VALUE	REORDER DATE	REORDER QTY	NOTES

JULY BUDGET

YEAR:

SOURCES OF INCOME SUMMARY	PROJECTED	ACTUAL	DIFFERENCE (+/-)
EXPENSES			
SAVINGS			
OTHER			

MONTHLY EXPENSE SUMMARY	PROJECTED	ACTUAL	DIFFERENCE (+/-)

JULY INCOME

DATE	SALES SOURCE	$ INCOME

JULY INCOME

DATE	SALES SOURCE	$ INCOME

JULY INCOME

DATE	SALES SOURCE	$ INCOME

JULY EXPENSES

DATE	DESCRIPTION	$ AMOUNT

JULY EXPENSES

DATE	DESCRIPTION	$ AMOUNT

JULY BUSINESS GOALS

_____
_____
_____
_____
_____
_____
_____

JULY MARKETING PLAN

CAMPAIGN/AUDIENCE	COST	NOTES

JULY SUPPLY INVENTORY

QTY	ITEM	$ VALUE	REORDER DATE	REORDER QTY	NOTES

AUGUST BUDGET

YEAR:

SOURCES OF INCOME SUMMARY	PROJECTED	ACTUAL	DIFFERENCE (+/-)
EXPENSES			
SAVINGS			
OTHER			

MONTHLY EXPENSE SUMMARY	PROJECTED	ACTUAL	DIFFERENCE (+/-)

AUGUST INCOME

DATE	SALES SOURCE	$ INCOME

AUGUST INCOME

DATE	SALES SOURCE	$ INCOME

AUGUST INCOME

DATE	SALES SOURCE	$ INCOME

AUGUST EXPENSES

DATE	DESCRIPTION	$ AMOUNT

AUGUST EXPENSES

DATE	DESCRIPTION	$ AMOUNT

AUGUST BUSINESS GOALS

_____

_____

_____

_____

_____

_____

_____

AUGUST MARKETING PLAN

CAMPAIGN/AUDIENCE	COST	NOTES

AUGUST SUPPLY INVENTORY

QTY	ITEM	$ VALUE	REORDER DATE	REORDER QTY	NOTES

SEPTEMBER BUDGET

YEAR:

SOURCES OF INCOME SUMMARY	PROJECTED	ACTUAL	DIFFERENCE (+/-)
EXPENSES			
SAVINGS			
OTHER			

MONTHLY EXPENSE SUMMARY	PROJECTED	ACTUAL	DIFFERENCE (+/-)

SEPTEMBER INCOME

DATE	SALES SOURCE	$ INCOME

SEPTEMBER INCOME

DATE	SALES SOURCE	$ INCOME

SEPTEMBER INCOME

DATE	SALES SOURCE	$ INCOME

SEPTEMBER EXPENSES

DATE	DESCRIPTION	$ AMOUNT

SEPTEMBER EXPENSES

DATE	DESCRIPTION	$ AMOUNT

SEPTEMBER BUSINESS GOALS

_____

_____

_____

_____

_____

_____

_____

SEPTEMBER MARKETING PLAN

CAMPAIGN/AUDIENCE	COST	NOTES

SEPTEMBER SUPPLY INVENTORY

QTY	ITEM	$ VALUE	REORDER DATE	REORDER QTY	NOTES

OCTOBER BUDGET

YEAR:

SOURCES OF INCOME SUMMARY	PROJECTED	ACTUAL	DIFFERENCE (+/-)
EXPENSES			
SAVINGS			
OTHER			

MONTHLY EXPENSE SUMMARY	PROJECTED	ACTUAL	DIFFERENCE (+/-)

OCTOBER INCOME

DATE	SALES SOURCE	$ INCOME

OCTOBER INCOME

DATE	SALES SOURCE	$ INCOME

OCTOBER INCOME

DATE	SALES SOURCE	$ INCOME

OCTOBER EXPENSES

DATE	DESCRIPTION	$ AMOUNT

OCTOBER EXPENSES

DATE	DESCRIPTION	$ AMOUNT

OCTOBER BUSINESS GOALS

_____
_____
_____
_____
_____
_____
_____

OCTOBER MARKETING PLAN

CAMPAIGN/AUDIENCE	COST	NOTES

OCTOBER SUPPLY INVENTORY

QTY	ITEM	$ VALUE	REORDER DATE	REORDER QTY	NOTES

NOVEMBER BUDGET

YEAR:

SOURCES OF INCOME SUMMARY	PROJECTED	ACTUAL	DIFFERENCE (+/-)
EXPENSES			
SAVINGS			
OTHER			

MONTHLY EXPENSE SUMMARY	PROJECTED	ACTUAL	DIFFERENCE (+/-)

NOVEMBER INCOME

DATE	SALES SOURCE	$ INCOME

NOVEMBER INCOME

DATE	SALES SOURCE	$ INCOME

NOVEMBER INCOME

DATE	SALES SOURCE	$ INCOME

NOVEMBER EXPENSES

DATE	DESCRIPTION	$ AMOUNT

NOVEMBER EXPENSES

DATE	DESCRIPTION	$ AMOUNT

NOVEMBER BUSINESS GOALS

_____

_____

_____

_____

_____

_____

NOVEMBER MARKETING PLAN

CAMPAIGN/AUDIENCE	COST	NOTES

NOVEMBER SUPPLY INVENTORY

QTY	ITEM	$ VALUE	REORDER DATE	REORDER QTY	NOTES

DECEMBER BUDGET

YEAR:

SOURCES OF INCOME SUMMARY	PROJECTED	ACTUAL	DIFFERENCE (+/-)
EXPENSES			
SAVINGS			
OTHER			

MONTHLY EXPENSE SUMMARY	PROJECTED	ACTUAL	DIFFERENCE (+/-)

DECEMBER INCOME

DATE	SALES SOURCE	$ INCOME

DECEMBER INCOME

DATE	SALES SOURCE	$ INCOME

DECEMBER INCOME

DATE	SALES SOURCE	$ INCOME

DECEMBER EXPENSES

DATE	DESCRIPTION	$ AMOUNT

DECEMBER EXPENSES

DATE	DESCRIPTION	$ AMOUNT

DECEMBER BUSINESS GOALS

_____
_____
_____
_____
_____
_____
_____
_____

DECEMBER MARKETING PLAN

CAMPAIGN/AUDIENCE	COST	NOTES

DECEMBER SUPPLY INVENTORY

QTY	ITEM	$ VALUE	REORDER DATE	REORDER QTY	NOTES

SUPPLIER CONTACT INFO

COMPANY	CONTACT	TELEPHONE	E-MAIL	WEBSITE

SUPPLIER CONTACT INFO

COMPANY	CONTACT	TELEPHONE	E-MAIL	WEBSITE

SUPPLIER CONTACT INFO

COMPANY	CONTACT	TELEPHONE	E-MAIL	WEBSITE

TAX DEDUCTIONS

DATE	DESCRIPTION	$ AMOUNT	NOTES

TAX DEDUCTIONS

DATE	DESCRIPTION	$ AMOUNT	NOTES

TAX DEDUCTIONS

DATE	DESCRIPTION	$ AMOUNT	NOTES

MILEAGE & GAS LOG

MAKE:			MODEL:			YEAR:
DATE	ODOMETER START	ODOMETER END	MILES DRIVEN	GAS $ BOUGHT	GAS PRICE	DESTINATION/PURPOSE

MILEAGE & GAS LOG

MAKE: MODEL: YEAR:

DATE	ODOMETER START	ODOMETER END	MILES DRIVEN	GAS $ BOUGHT	GAS PRICE	DESTINATION/PURPOSE

MILEAGE & GAS LOG

MAKE:		MODEL:			YEAR:	
DATE	ODOMETER START	ODOMETER END	MILES DRIVEN	GAS $ BOUGHT	GAS PRICE	DESTINATION/PURPOSE

MILEAGE & GAS LOG

MAKE:		MODEL:				YEAR:
DATE	ODOMETER START	ODOMETER END	MILES DRIVEN	GAS $ BOUGHT	GAS PRICE	DESTINATION/PURPOSE

MILEAGE & GAS LOG

MAKE:		MODEL:			YEAR:	
DATE	ODOMETER START	ODOMETER END	MILES DRIVEN	GAS $ BOUGHT	GAS PRICE	DESTINATION/PURPOSE

MILEAGE & GAS LOG

MAKE:		MODEL:			YEAR:	
DATE	ODOMETER START	ODOMETER END	MILES DRIVEN	GAS $ BOUGHT	GAS PRICE	DESTINATION/PURPOSE

MILEAGE & GAS LOG

MAKE:			MODEL:			YEAR:
DATE	ODOMETER START	ODOMETER END	MILES DRIVEN	GAS $ BOUGHT	GAS PRICE	DESTINATION/PURPOSE

MILEAGE & GAS LOG

MAKE:		MODEL:			YEAR:	
DATE	ODOMETER START	ODOMETER END	MILES DRIVEN	GAS $ BOUGHT	GAS PRICE	DESTINATION/PURPOSE

MILEAGE & GAS LOG

MAKE: MODEL: YEAR:

DATE	ODOMETER START	ODOMETER END	MILES DRIVEN	GAS $ BOUGHT	GAS PRICE	DESTINATION/PURPOSE

MILEAGE & GAS LOG

MAKE:		MODEL:				YEAR:
DATE	ODOMETER START	ODOMETER END	MILES DRIVEN	GAS $ BOUGHT	GAS PRICE	DESTINATION/PURPOSE

MILEAGE & GAS LOG

MAKE:		MODEL:			YEAR:	
DATE	ODOMETER START	ODOMETER END	MILES DRIVEN	GAS $ BOUGHT	GAS PRICE	DESTINATION/PURPOSE

MILEAGE & GAS LOG

MAKE:		MODEL:		YEAR:		
DATE	ODOMETER START	ODOMETER END	MILES DRIVEN	GAS $ BOUGHT	GAS PRICE	DESTINATION/PURPOSE

MILEAGE & GAS LOG

MAKE:		MODEL:				YEAR:
DATE	ODOMETER START	ODOMETER END	MILES DRIVEN	GAS $ BOUGHT	GAS PRICE	DESTINATION/PURPOSE

MILEAGE & GAS LOG

MAKE:		MODEL:				YEAR:
DATE	ODOMETER START	ODOMETER END	MILES DRIVEN	GAS $ BOUGHT	GAS PRICE	DESTINATION/PURPOSE

MILEAGE & GAS LOG

MAKE:		MODEL:				YEAR:
DATE	ODOMETER START	ODOMETER END	MILES DRIVEN	GAS $ BOUGHT	GAS PRICE	DESTINATION/PURPOSE

CPSIA information can be obtained
at www.ICGtesting.com
Printed in the USA
LVHW100728141119
636961LV00043B/4727/P